Strange Mitch

GW00649051

Ghosts, Legends & Curiosities of Mitcham in
Surrey / South London

By James Clark

Second (revised) edition

Shadowtime Publishing

STRANGE MITCHAM

First published 2002.

Second (revised) edition published 2011.

Published by Shadowtime Publishing, Mitcham, Surrey, UK.

Printed by www.lulu.com

ISBN: 978-0-9541995-1-7

Dedicated to my parents, for everything.

STRANGE MITCHAM

Praise for the first edition of *Strange Mitcham*:

'Very many thanks for sending me so promptly your excellent book *Strange Mitcham*. I have enjoyed reading it (twice, so far!) so much.' (Jeanne Dworak)

'I would like to say how much my wife and I enjoyed your fascinating book. It makes amazing reading, and we eagerly await the sequel.' (Phil Rosier)

'I recently obtained a copy of your book *Strange Mitcham*, which I read with enormous interest. Despite having lived in or around Mitcham for 60 years, I learnt an awful lot that I had not known before […] I do hope your sequel comes out soon.' (Christopher Patterson)

'*Strange Mitcham* is a very enjoyable read indeed. Do not, for one moment, think that you need to know about Mitcham and the surrounding areas as you don't. […] I strongly suggest that this book would be a welcome addition to any Fortean's bookshelf. Get it today.' (Dave McMann)

'A useful addition to local paranormal data.' (The Travel and Earth Mysteries Society)

'Lovely book.' (Charles Miller)

'Excellent book!' (Neil Arnold)

'An excellent, and well put together, read.' (Gordon Sinclair)

'Great book, can't seem to put it down!' (Julie Huscroft)

Contents

Acknowledgements

I am deeply grateful to the following without whose help I could not have written this: Pauline Barrell (Parish Secretary, Mitcham Parish Church), Lionel Beer, Martin Boyle (Warden, Mitcham Common), Tony Dow, Della Edwards, Sue Gardner, Jeremy Harte (curator, Bourne Hall Museum), Ann Hopkins, Ronald John, Susan Maxwell, Merton Local Studies Centre, Eric Montague, Rev. John Shepherd, Christine Stokes, Kim Teague and Clive Whichelow.

My thanks also go to my father and brother for reading the proofs and suggesting improvements, my mother for helping me with the photographs and www.prehocsolutions.co.uk for invaluable technical assistance.

(Apologies to anyone I have overlooked.)

All photographs come from the author's collection. The cover image shows the obelisk at the junction of Madeira Road and Cricket Green, Mitcham.

Map contains Ordnance Survey data © Contains Crown copyright and database right 2011.

Introduction

Mitcham is old. The very name is thought to derive from an Anglo-Saxon word meaning 'the big home', and the discovery of Neolithic flint tools suggests that land clearance and cultivation, and probably settlement, was underway in this part of the River Wandle's valley even further back in time – as long ago as 3,000 BC. Given how long people have been living around here then, it is hardly surprising that the area has accumulated many strange stories over the years.

The curiosities described in the following pages include encounters with ghosts, rumours of a secret tunnel, a miraculous spring, attacks by a demonic bogeyman, and much else. In one or two cases, the entries deal with sites that lie just on the outside edge of Mitcham proper (e.g. Merton Priory). I make no apology for including these sites however, since they are simply far too interesting to be left out!

Strange Mitcham is offered as part of Project Albion, an ongoing programme by ASSAP (the Association for the Scientific Study of Anomalous Phenomena) to record and collate mysteries and folklore from all across the British Isles in what has been called a 'Domesday Book of the paranormal'. Further information about ASSAP is available from their website at www.assap.org.

The first edition of *Strange Mitcham* appeared as a printed booklet in 2002. For this revised edition, as well as making the content available as an eBook, I have taken the opportunity to update a few chapters with details that have come to light over the past few years. During those same years I have also written a sequel to *Strange Mitcham*. Titled *Mysterious Mitcham*, the sequel includes many more stories about the odd side of this town. For more information about this and about my other books please see my website at www.james-clark.co.uk.

I hope that you enjoy reading the following stories and discovering some of this old town's hidden secrets....

James Clark, 2011

Map legend:

1. The Haunting of Rose Cottage
2. The Phantom Cyclist of Mitcham Common
3. Invasion of the Body Snatchers
4. A Secret Tunnel?
5. Queen for a Year
6. 'Dead Man's Lane'
7. Mitcham Parish Church
8. The Treasure of a Gypsy Queen
9. The Obelisk
10. Ghost Lights
11. Spring-Heeled Jack
12. Maiden Hill – A Lost Tumulus?
13. The Curse of Merton Priory
14. Everett's Place

Map

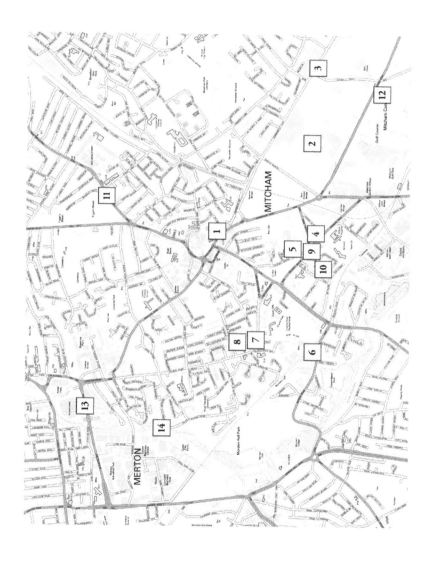

The Haunting of Rose Cottage

Today it is known simply as 13 Commonside East. This narrow house stands at right angles to its neighbours, at the end of a short row of historic buildings opposite the Three Kings Pond. Thought to date back to the late 18th century, it has seen many strange incidents over the years.

The story of the haunting of Rose Cottage is a little confused though, probably as a result of continual retellings and exaggerations. For instance, there is a vague reference to a malevolent spirit that terrorised the occupants at some date prior to the 1920s. This spirit would supposedly race up and down the stairs, making a dreadful racket akin to someone stamping around in hobnailed boots.

Whatever this was, it seems unlikely to have been the phantom lady seen there during the 1920s. This pleasant apparition appeared shortly after Christmas one year, startling the then occupier, Mrs Burton. It was at about 10 o'clock at night, as Mrs Burton was walking down the stairs carrying her husband's slippers, that she saw a stately middle-aged lady walk from the drawing room into the dining room. The figure appeared to be perfectly solid but when Mrs Burton and her husband looked to see who was there, all they found was an empty room and a strong scent of lavender.

For some reason, this ghost became popularly known as Lady Jane. People have disagreed over her appearance, and she is variously described as wearing the fashions of '60 years' earlier (i.e. c.1860) and of the 14th century. (Presumably, during the repeated recording of the story, somebody misread '60 years' as '600 years', or vice versa.)

Mrs Burton's aunt, who lived in Rose Cottage before her, had spoken of hearing inexplicable noises and there were rumours that previous occupiers had also seen Lady Jane, so the above may not have been the first sighting. It does seem to have been the last however, although other supernatural happenings continued to occur.

Mrs Burton would sometimes sense a presence when there was nobody around. On one occasion, she and her husband heard heavy footsteps overhead (hobnailed boots again?) but when they hurried upstairs there was nothing to be seen.

When the council numbered the buildings in Commonside East, a number 13 was hung on Rose Cottage's door. This seems to have irritated whatever strange forces were in residence for shortly afterwards a number of poltergeist-like effects were reported. Apparently, a heavy drawer was sent crashing to the ground and the contents of various cupboards were flung about. (It should be said, however, that these particular episodes were later claimed to have been exaggerated by journalists.) Eventually, the number was removed from the door. This seemed to do the trick as the violent episodes ceased, although strange noises continued to be heard.

A possible cause of these sounds was discovered by Mrs Burton one day when her young children were playing in the drawing room and the floor seemed to move. Workmen were called in to investigate and when they removed the floor they discovered an ancient well. Had the noises been nothing more than the echoes of small stones and bits of dirt dropping down into its depths?

Certainly, the noises stopped when the well was filled in, as did all reports of ghostly activity for many years.

The 1990s

In 1977, the building was substantially rebuilt, although its essential character was retained, and the following year it became the registered offices of Drummond Design and Building Services Ltd. Perhaps the building work reawakened something because in 1998 Drummond's Mrs Susan Maxwell told me of a number of strange experiences she had had whilst employed there.

On numerous occasions, she would become aware of a powerful scent of lavender as she was working. (Remember that the scent of lavender was associated with the apparition seen in the 1920s.)

Often, files and stationery would go missing, sometimes for months on end, and then suddenly turn up again in the most obvious places. There had apparently been a running joke among some staff that the ghost was responsible for these disappearances.

In the mid-1990s, Mrs Maxwell was alone in the building, typing letters when she heard an 'almighty crash'.

'I thought perhaps a wall had collapsed or ceiling fell down,' she said. 'I checked all rooms and outside the building but nothing had fallen. I was quite frightened by this experience.'

Her sister worked there too and she also experienced a few odd events. One time, after everyone else had gone home, she discovered that the front door was jammed firmly shut. Unable to leave, she eventually telephoned her in-laws and persuaded them to come to her rescue. When they arrived she threw the keys to them out of a window and they tried to open the door from the outside. It opened for them without any trouble whatsoever.

On a separate occasion, Mrs Maxwell attempted to open the front door one morning and discovered that her key would not fit the lock.

'It was like something was behind it. I could not get the key in at all. I waited for a while until my colleague came, who also tried to open the door with his key but [he] had the same experience.'

They were discussing breaking the door down when Mrs Maxwell's sister turned up.

'I said to my colleague,' recalled Mrs Maxwell, '"Wouldn't it be funny if she opened the door?" She did without any problem. We were totally amazed. We never had a problem with [the door] again, and there is no explanation.'

The most dramatic incident Mrs Maxwell experienced occurred one day as she was book-keeping: 'Suddenly my glass of water moved. I looked in total amazement and then it moved again.'

She concluded by saying that she certainly felt a presence of some sort within Rose Cottage, and that she believed it to be 'friendly but mischievous'.

Since then, Rose Cottage has changed hands and at the time of writing (January 2011) I am unaware of any further ghostly activity having been reported.

A dark history

It is not known what lies behind the strange incidents in this otherwise attractive building, but haunted houses often turn out to have interesting histories. In this respect Rose Cottage is no exception.

One old rumour has it that, long ago, a murder was committed either within Rose Cottage itself or in its neighbour, the since-demolished number 15, and that the corpse was disposed of down a well in the house. Also, in 1894, a man named James Canham Read was arrested in this building for the murder of one of his mistresses, Florrie Dennis. Read was subsequently hanged for his crime (see 'Appendix: The Southend Murderer'). The murder weapon, a revolver, was never found and popular belief had it that the killer threw it down a well inside the house where it has lain ever since.

Presumably these references to a well concern the same one that Mrs Burton later discovered in the drawing room.

Perhaps it is a shame that the workmen Mrs Burton hired did not search the well's depths for rusting revolvers or ancient skeletons before filling it in. If they had, might they have found an explanation for the haunting of Rose Cottage?

The Phantom Cyclist of Mitcham Common

Seven Islands pond on Mitcham Common is not natural. Rather, it owes its existence to a series of old gravel pits that eventually became filled with water. During the 1920s and 1930s it was a very picturesque feature on the common and was used for boating and swimming. These days, it is far too shallow for such activities and so there are no sailors or swimmers around. There may, however, be a phantom cyclist!

This apparition was encountered by a gentleman named Tony Dow, and I initially discovered his account on two internet sites that deal with the paranormal: 'O'Neill's Ghostories' (sic) Casements Library' and 'Obiwan's UFO-Free Paranormal Page'.

When I wrote about this story in the first edition of *Strange Mitcham* I stated that I had been unable to contact Mr Dow to obtain any further information. Since then, I have been in touch with him and he kindly provided some additional details about his encounter.

STRANGE MITCHAM

It happened between around 1990 and 1992 while Mr Dow was working the night shift as a computer operator for a firm based on the Willow Lane Industrial Estate. He would not finish work until around two or three a.m., and when he did finally leave for home it was his habit to take a short cut across Mitcham Common.

The common was normally deathly silent at that time of the morning but on this occasion, as he walked past Seven Islands, Dow heard a distant noise. As he listened, the sound grew louder and louder and he eventually recognised it as the sound of a bicycle riding across grass. It seemed to be approaching him, so he turned to look. It was indeed a bicycle.

Initially, he was relieved that that was all the noise had been, but then something struck him as a little odd. Although this was the early hours of the morning, the boy riding the bike could not have been more than seven or eight years old.

The young cyclist drew ever closer, staring directly into Dow's eyes. It was a remarkably fixed gaze, and one that began to unnerve the older man.

When the boy reached him, he cycled past without a word, his eyes staying locked on Dow's, even turning his head to look back over his shoulder, all the time staring fixedly. It was hard to understand how he could control the bike like that.

By now Dow was feeling distinctly uneasy, but what followed really scared him. The boy cycled steadily on, still staring back, closer and closer to the pond and then out onto the surface of the water. He did not sink, but just continued on.

'The bike was on the surface of the water,' wrote Dow, 'and there was now no sound of the chain or the wheels turning.'

As he watched the unsettling apparition travel across the pond and on into the distance, something else now struck Dow as odd. The boy was dressed entirely in white, and his bicycle too was white.

At last, Dow's nerve broke. He bolted and ran home. For weeks afterwards, the incident preyed on his mind as he wondered whether he might have seen the ghost of a young boy who had drowned in the pond. Perhaps, he speculated, the boy had been cycling across the pond's frozen surface one winter's day when the ice had cracked beneath him.

(During my original research for *Strange Mitcham* I tried to find out if a young boy had ever drowned in Seven Islands pond but I was unsuccessful. In 2005, however, I was contacted by someone who informed me that her mother's brother had drowned here in 1939, when he was ten years old. For more details on this, see my sequel to *Strange Mitcham*, entitled *Mysterious Mitcham*. The sequel also contains another ghost story from the vicinity of Seven Islands.)

Before his encounter, Dow had been a confirmed sceptic on the subject of ghosts, but he has never forgotten this experience. He never tried to research the incident though, for fear of what he might discover.

Afterwards he stopped walking across Mitcham Common in the early hours of the morning, instead taking a route along Cedars Avenue. It took a little longer to get home but he just could not face the possibility of another meeting with that sinister cyclist in white.

Invasion of the Body Snatchers

A trail known as the 'Workhouse Path' once began at Blue Houses Bridge (beside the intersection of Cedars Avenue, Croydon Road and Carshalton Road) and ran across Mitcham Common. The beginning of this path is long gone now but on the other side of the modern Cedars Avenue, by the roundabout, a narrow strip of rocky earth heads east into the bushes.

How closely the present path follows the older one is difficult to say, but it is a pleasant walk and as the path widens, cutting through the tall grass, traffic noise quickly fades to a distant murmur, to be replaced by birdsong, rustling leaves and the occasional scurrying of something in the undergrowth.

Until 1838 the site at the end of this path was occupied by Mitcham Workhouse, hence the path's old name. A red brick building with a prominent clock, the workhouse had been erected in 1782 to provide housing for Mitcham's poor and destitute and to offer shelter to tramps. Permission had been specially granted to build on what is common ground because the workhouse was seen as being humanitarian and in the public interest.

There was, however, a very dark side to the place.

Amateur historian Tom Francis (d. 1953) recorded in his notes on *Old Mitcham* that he had heard tell of body snatchers working these grim premises, taking the corpses of unfortunate souls who passed away there and selling them for 'anatomical purposes', i.e. to be dissected by doctors and medical students.

Prior to the 1832 Anatomy Act, the only corpses the medical profession could legally get their hands on were those of hanged murderers, but these averaged only 20–30 per year. And at that time few people would voluntarily leave their body to science because of the belief that being buried incomplete would cost them their place in Heaven. So the medical profession's demand for the so-called resurrectionists' services was great.

Surprisingly, body snatching was not actually illegal. Bodies were not considered to be property and so taking them could not be equated with stealing. If caught, body snatchers could only be tried for relatively minor offences such as breaking and entering or offending public morals.

Nevertheless, there must have been considerable danger involved in their work. Whenever body snatching exploits came to light somewhere, there was an explosion of public outrage, and anyone exposed would have faced the wrath of the mob.

On the other hand, there was considerable money to be made. According to Francis, the snatchers in Mitcham typically worked for a retaining fee of £50 and earned themselves a further £9 per cadaver.

In 1941, the 18th-century workhouse building was destroyed during an air raid. I am not aware of any ghostly tales from the site (which can be found at the north-east corner of the junction of Windmill Road and Commonside East) but with all those restless souls denied a proper burial, who knows?

A Secret Tunnel?

There is a long-standing rumour that a secret tunnel runs underneath Cranmer Green.

The entrance is supposed to be hidden behind a movable flagstone in the cellar of the Canons. This attractive white building (shown above) stands just to the north of Cranmer Green and is much older than its Victorian features at first suggest. Major alterations have been made to it throughout the years but it was originally built during the reign of King Charles II and is more than 300 years old.

It was built on the site of an even older structure – also called the Canons – which seems to have been part of a farm belonging to the Augustinian priory of St Mary Overie at Southwark. (This was before the priory lost its Mitcham estates during the dissolution of the monasteries in the mid-16th century.) Further back in history, the land may have been held by the canons of Bayeux, who are believed to have owned the manor of Mitcham during the 11th century.

Several people claim to have seen the tunnel entrance although none of them was brave enough to venture inside. The tunnel, it is said, leads south, under Madeira Road, Cranmer Green and Cranmer Road. It would have opened into the cellar of Rectory House, which stood close to the site of the present-day Wilson Hospital. Unfortunately, Rectory House (later known as The Cranmers) was demolished in 1928 so the tunnel, if it exists, presumably leads only to a dead-end now.

Why would anyone have built such a tunnel in the first place?

One suggestion is that it was used by the monks at Merton Priory but this seems unlikely given the distance separating the Priory from the Canons.

Another theory is that it was intended as an escape route for Roman Catholic priests. During the latter part of the 16th century Roman Catholicism was considered subversive as it placed allegiance to the Pope – a foreign power – above allegiance to the British Crown. For a time, the perceived threat was taken so seriously that the practice of Roman Catholicism was declared treasonable and approximately 200 people were executed throughout the country for refusing to give up the 'Old Faith'.

Because of this, hiding places (known as 'priests' holes') and escape routes became common features of Catholic homes, in case the authorities caught the owners in the act of celebrating Mass. Since the present Canons was not built until the late 17th century, it would seem that the tunnel, if it really was built for this purpose, actually pre-dates the existing building.

In 1970, historians were given a wonderful opportunity to investigate the legend when a North Sea gas main was laid from Mitcham to Croydon. As members of Merton Historical Society watched, a huge trench was dug through the Canons' grounds and across Cranmer Green. However, the only tunnel-like structure revealed was a small brick culvert apparently connected to the Canons' pond. This result was disappointing for those who believe the legend but it cannot be said to be conclusive.

Stories of secret tunnels do occasionally turn out to be based in fact. For example, in their 1995 booklet *More Mysterious Wimbledon*, authors Ruth

STRANGE MITCHAM

Murphy and Clive Whichelow describe several factual tunnels close to Mitcham, such as one running under Merton High Street linking the Lord Nelson public house with Haydons Road.

It is possible that the rumoured hidden tunnel under Cranmer Green may yet prove to be very real.

(Above: Cranmer Green from near the Wilson Hospital, looking back towards the Canons.)

(For more stories of nearby tunnels, including the claim that a secret passage connects Mitcham's Vestry Hall to a nearby pub, see my *Mysterious Mitcham*.)

Queen for a Year

Until recently, Mitcham celebrated the beginning of spring with the crowning of a May Queen. Her reign would last for just one year, during which time she would take her place of honour on a float to the annual carnival, and carry out official duties such as delivering presents to the elderly and opening fetes.

The origins of ceremonies such as this are believed to lie in the murky depths of prehistory, when the Celts celebrated the feast of Beltane. Celts considered May Day to be the first day of summer – the day when the Earth at last awoke from her long winter sleep – and they would celebrate the occasion with eating, drinking and dancing. Presiding over these riotous affairs was a May Queen, selected from among the young ladies of the community, who wore a costume decorated with leaves representing Nature's creative power.

Mitcham's ceremony was not quite so ancient but was nevertheless well established, being a late-Victorian revival. I went along to watch events in 1999.

The festival began on Three Kings Piece, where all the participating children took their places for the procession. To the accompaniment of a marching band, the previous year's May Queen and her consort, Prince Charming, led their retinue through the town centre's streets. Behind them walked the Banner Queen, followed by Maid Marian and Robin Hood. Next came the Fairy Queen and her fairies; the Maid of Honour Queen, her attendant and the Maids of Honour; the Peach Queen and her Peaches; the Forget-me-not Queen, her attendant and the Forget-me-nots; the Rosebud Queen and her Buds; and the Primrose Queen, her attendant and the Primroses. Following all these marched the Characters (who would differ from one year to the next – in 1999 they were Peter Pan, Tinkerbell and Sooty). And behind the Characters came the Garland Queen and her Garland Girls, the Crown Bearer, the soon-to-be Prince Charming and the Lady-in-Waiting. At the very end of the line, escorted by her trainbearers, came the May Queen Elect.

Altogether, approximately 70 children in full costume processed in stately fashion to the Canons for the crowning ceremony. This would usually take place on the grass in front of that 17th-century building but, English weather being the way it is, the proceedings would occasionally be moved into the neighbouring leisure centre.

At the Canons, the children were announced one by one as they entered and took their places. The retiring May Queen climbed onto a flower-decked dais and took the throne as her retinue assembled about her. Once everyone was ready, the parish vicar offered an opening prayer. Next, the retiring Prince Charming and May Queen gave their farewell speeches and, after receiving a presentation from the Mayor of Merton, they surrendered their seats and moved from the dais to the nearby Flower Arch.

The new Queen and Prince were then invited to take the vacated seats. The May Queen Elect ascended the throne for the first time and, to the applause of the watching crowd, she was crowned by the Mayor. As with the seasons, the old was replaced with the new and the cycle was ready to begin again.

It was a charming ceremony and one that well illustrated the way that this town was stubbornly holding on to its identity in the face of London's expansion. For a few short hours at the beginning of each May, Mitcham's busy urban centre would be transformed into what could have been a little village green, albeit one with some rather bemused onlookers.

Sadly, the tradition now appears to have faded away. It would be a great shame were it to be lost forever and I hope it may yet return.

'Dead Man's Lane' and Mitcham Parish Church

Once, people knew it as 'Dead Man's Lane' – just the title to conjure up thoughts of restless phantoms and prompt a lonely traveller to glance nervously around. No wonder Morden Road used to be regarded with superstitious fear!

The uneasy atmosphere there was recorded in Lt-Col. H.F. Bidder's 1926 collection of essays on *Old Mitcham*. In one of these essays, Sir Thomas Cato Worsfold (Mitcham's first MP and an amateur historian) wrote that he still clearly remembered 'the "creepy" feeling one had in the dusk or at night walking down the Morden Road by the side of Ravensbury Park'.

Although the occasional human bone was indeed unearthed in the area, the reason for what Worsfold called the 'gruesome title' had long been lost to history. It was not until the late 19th century that excavations by the Bidder family revealed the forgotten truth, that 'Dead Man's Lane' was a path through an ancient burial ground.

Between 1888 and 1922, excavations uncovered some 230 graves, and it is probable that a number of others have been destroyed over time, or else lie still waiting to be discovered. Many graves were those of Anglo-Saxon warriors, who had been buried with their weapons and valuables, and from the artefacts found the site has been dated to around AD 450–600.

Most of the graves were discovered to either side of Morden Road, between Mitcham Station in the east and Ravensbury Park in the west. Others have been found further afield, the most northerly being uncovered close to the site of Mitcham's Parish Church of St Peter and St Paul.

This may be more than coincidence….

A pagan past?

Local historian E.N. Montague has suggested that the missionaries responsible for converting Mitcham's early inhabitants to Christianity may have erected a cross or small chapel close to this already sacred burial ground in a deliberate attempt to absorb the pagan religion into their own. Such tactics of conversion-by-stealth were documented by the scholar Bede (c. AD 673–735) in his most famous work: *The Ecclesiastical History of the English People.*

Bede quotes Pope Gregory I's instructions to Augustine of Canterbury, which were conveyed by Mellitus when the latter came to England at the beginning of the 7th century:

> *We wish to inform you that we have given careful thought to the affairs of the English, and have come to the conclusion that the temples of the idols among that people should on no account be destroyed. The idols are to be destroyed, but the temples themselves are to be aspersed with holy water, altars set up in them, and relics deposited there.*

For if these temples are well built, they must be purified from the worship of demons and dedicated to the service of the true God. In this way, we hope that the people, seeing that their temples are not destroyed, may abandon their error and, flocking more readily to their accustomed resorts, may come to know and adore the true God.

It may be, therefore, that Mitcham's Parish Church is the latest incarnation of a holy site dating back around 1,500 years!

Of course, the church that currently stands here is much younger than that. Although it does incorporate some ancient features – such as the base of the tower, which dates from c. AD 1250 – the bulk of it was built in 1819–22. Despite its relative youth, however, it has some interesting idiosyncrasies of its own.

Curious stone carvings

In *The Gentleman's Magazine* in 1821, a letter from 'E.I.C.' savagely attacked the church's architectural design, finding fault with just about all he could see. After venting his distaste for everything from the ceiling mouldings to the shape of the doors, the writer turned his attention to the carved stone faces adorning the windows on the church's outside walls:

[...] the subjects they are intended to represent are inexplicable [...] But perhaps none are equal to a pair in the upper story of the vestry, which, on account of the singularity of the association, deserve to be noticed as, perhaps, the greatest absurdity ever invented for embellishments of a church. The first of these heads is furnished with a grotesque countenance, large ears, and a conspicuous pair of horns, and is intended, no doubt, for the eternal enemy of mankind, whilst the second, strange to tell, is a mitred bishop. The first time, I believe, the head of the Devil has formed an embellishment of a Christian church [...]

These heads can still be seen today. The 'Devil' and the Bishop referred to above look out from either side of the window above the door at the south-east corner. Many other heads can be seen beside the church's windows.

One especially hideous head is that of an old woman, which glares out from the right-hand-side of the second window from the west end. Montague, in his guide to the church, tells us of a tradition attached to this stony crone. Supposedly, the mason who was sculpting these corbels had to put up with constant criticism of his work from a woman who lived nearby. (Perhaps she was a relative of 'E.I.C.'!) At last, the poor fellow's irritation got the better of him and this was his revenge – an unflattering caricature of his tormentor.

The Treasure of a Gypsy Queen

Legend has it that a 'Gypsy Queen' lies buried in Mitcham, and that hidden in her grave is a fortune in gold and jewellery. As unlikely as this sounds, traditions do often prove to have some truth in them, however distorted this may have become with age. Investigation reveals this to be such a tale.

It seems that the queen in question was a 35-year-old woman by the name of Sophie Karpath. Sophie was the daughter of Nicholas Tscheiron, chief of the Gillisham tribe of Gypsies, which in 1911 was camped in a field at Beddington Corner on the edge of Mitcham Common.

Sophie had become seriously ill with pneumonia and after suffering for several weeks in her husband's tent, she was taken to Carshalton Hospital. Tragically, the doctors were unable to save her and she died there.

Her body was taken to Mitcham Parish Church for burial. There, an elaborate funeral ceremony took place, attended not only by her grieving relatives and the other members of her tribe, but also by crowds of curious locals, eager to watch this exotic spectacle.

In accordance with Gypsy custom, Sophie's body was dressed in fine clothes: three new frocks, the outer one being scarlet, striped purple stockings and a new pair of silver-buckled shoes. Her hair was carefully arranged and she was adorned with valuable jewellery. Gold coins worth 20 shillings were put in her ears, rings around her fingers and necklaces of hundred-franc pieces were draped around her neck.

A solemn procession conveyed her oaken coffin to the chapel. There, the coffin lid was removed and Sophie was seated in an upright position, holding a lighted candle in each hand. For the next hour and a half the Gypsies paid their last respects, throwing coins (mainly of gold) into her lap until, at last, she was taken to her grave.

STRANGE MITCHAM

After the funeral, there was a distasteful incident when the gentleman who had acted as interpreter throughout the service accosted the verger, complaining that he had not been paid. He wanted to borrow a spade and shovel to dig up the coffin and take his fee from the deceased's jewellery! His request was, of course, refused.

This then would seem to be the story of Mitcham's buried treasure. The obvious question is, does it still lay here?

Many think this unlikely, believing that greed must have long ago overcome respect for the dead. But nobody knows for sure.

The grave certainly exists but when I was originally shown the site the vicar was rightly anxious to prevent its desecration by would-be treasure-hunters so I will refrain from disclosing its exact location to ensure that Sophie Karpath – Mitcham's 'Gypsy Queen' – continues to rest in peace.

The Obelisk

Not far from the Canons, at the busy junction of Madeira Road and Cricket Green, a strange object juts up from the pavement. It is a tall, sand-coloured obelisk – a tapering pillar capped with a pyramid.

Built of bricks and faced with Roman cement, the obelisk bears the following weatherworn inscription:

In

grateful recollection

of the goodness of

God

through whose favor (sic)

water has been provided

for this neighbourhood

God opened the rock

and the waters gushed

out; they ran in dry

places like a river

Psalm CV. v.41

He turneth dry ground

into water springs

Psalm CVII. v.35

Let everything that hath

breath praise the Lord

Psalm CL. v.6

A Fountain shall water

the valley

Joel III. v.18

Beneath this is carved a date: 'Sept. 25th, 1822'.

The story behind this monument is that the summers of 1821 and 1822 had seen remarkably little rain in Mitcham and the local people – most of who relied on shallow wells for their water – found themselves facing a drought. In previous years, such a problem had been overcome by obtaining water from the River Wandle but times had changed and pollution from the new tanneries at Beddington had rendered that water undrinkable.

In the face of hardship, religious feelings often become more acute, and when a natural artesian well was discovered in the corner of the Canons' grounds, parishioners interpreted the event as miraculous, a sure sign of God's compassion. Their gratitude was given solid form when the Revd. Richard Cranmer, son of the lord of the manor of Mitcham, erected this obelisk.

Perhaps by offering thanks in this highly visible way the townspeople hoped to ensure a long existence for their new and life-saving well. If so, they were to be disappointed. Records show that once the obelisk was completed the spring promptly dried up.

'A Mitcham Whisper'

By the late 19th century, Mitcham had acquired a reputation for itself among the surrounding villages. Unfortunately, it was not a particularly flattering one.

It was said that the 'common herd' among Mitcham's residents was incapable of communicating in any fashion other a loud bellow. Walford (1884) records the use of the popular expression 'a Mitcham whisper' to sarcastically refer to such uncouth shouting.

Ghost Lights

One bright Sunday afternoon in either the spring or summer of 1975, two schoolgirls had a strange experience that left them wondering, is there life after death?

At the time, Sue Gardner was 14 years old and lived in Carshalton. Every Sunday after lunch, she would travel to Mitcham with her school-friend 'Alison' (pseudonym). Here, they would visit Alison's paternal grandmother and aunt at their home in Bramcote Avenue (below), a short distance to the south of the Cricket Green. In 1975, however, Alison's grandmother – 'Mrs Bridger' (pseudonym) – died of cancer, so their visits stopped for a while.

This particular afternoon was the girls' first visit to the house since Mrs Bridger had passed away. As they got closer, both were feeling slightly apprehensive. At the front door, they were greeted by Alison's 'Aunt Mary' (pseudonym), and the girls went into the front room to sit down.

STRANGE MITCHAM

'We would always sit in the front room,' recalled Sue, 'where Mrs Bridger had her own armchair and likewise Aunt Mary, either side of the fireplace; Mary on the left, and Alison and myself on the sofa against the far wall.'

The atmosphere was tinged with sadness, and Sue remembers how aware she was of Mrs Bridger's vacant armchair. Then, as she lowered herself onto the sofa, she noticed an odd round patch of light about six feet [1.8 metres] in front of her.

'It was inevitable that we should glance over at the empty chair as we took our usual seats,' said Sue. 'On the right-hand corner of the back of her chair, there seemed to emanate a circle of light, with one quarter of it "missing", as if hiding behind the chair, or even inside it.'

'I blinked several times and looked away, as I couldn't quite believe what I was seeing. I would look back at intervals, assuming it was a trick of the light, but every time I did it was still there.

'It couldn't have been more than five or six inches [13–15 cm] across, was white all the way through, and was quite bright, in spite of the sunny day.'

A few moments later, Sue became aware of a second luminous disc in the room, this one inside a china cabinet that stood behind the empty armchair, in an alcove beside the fireplace. This second light was on the back of the interior of the cabinet, half-hidden behind one of the displayed plates.

Both lights were bright, white and approximately the same size. The only noticeable difference was that the light in the cabinet was not quite as intense as that on the chair.

What was bizarre, however, was that there were no obvious light sources (indoors or outdoors) or reflective surfaces that might be responsible for the bright discs. It was as though they were actually being produced from within the chair and the cabinet!

Sue and Alison stayed at Aunt Mary's for between two and three hours, but nobody said anything about the strange discs, so Sue was not sure if anyone else could see them. The lights remained clearly visible the entire time and did not change their position in the slightest (as might have been expected over such a long period had they been caused by the sun). They were still there when the girls eventually left.

Outside, Sue told Alison what she had seen: 'On the way home, I mentioned it to my friend, who was easily frightened by such things, and normally of a ruddy complexion. I've never seen her look so pale, as I described what I'd seen – she had seen it too – then I knew it wasn't my imagination.'

Sue believes that the lights were a sign from Mrs Bridger. She feels that the old lady was 'letting us know that she was still around and that there really is a "beyond".'

Spring-Heeled Jack

Background

During the mid-1830s, dark rumours began to circulate in the villages surrounding London. Some evil being – a 'ghost, imp or devil' according to *The Morning Chronicle* of 10 January 1838 – was haunting the night, and his terrifying visitations were frightening people out of their senses. Some put his strange attacks down to the pranks of a malicious band of young aristocrats impersonating a supernatural entity, but others firmly believed there was a genuine demon wandering abroad.

Early descriptions of this mysterious figure vary considerably, and this must have added to the confusion and fear. Witnesses described it as a large white animal (typically a bear or a bull); a ghost; a figure in full shining armour (somewhat like the ghost of Hamlet's father); a black-cloaked fiend or even the Devil himself. Was this demon able to change his form? Or might there be more than one?

As the days and nights passed, the stories escalated. It was said that several women had been scared quite literally to their deaths, and that the bodies of children had been found ripped to pieces by monstrous claws. The reported attacks seemed to follow a pattern: the assailant would leap from the shadows without warning, commit his crime and then bound away back into the darkness. Those leaps, people said, were unnatural. No mortal man could jump that far or that high. Such claims fuelled speculation as to the attacker's supernatural origin.

Those people unwilling to believe such nonsense asserted that he must wear boots with India-rubber soles, or that there was some sort of spring-loaded mechanism in the boots' heels, although the same people hesitated to provide details as to how such a device might work.

As the stories grew increasingly lurid, the attacks were reported more frequently and from an ever-widening area. By around 1838, the fiend had reportedly struck on Tooting Bec Common. (For details of this and other Spring-Heeled Jack sightings within the London Borough of Wandsworth, see my *Haunted Wandsworth*.)

The progress of the reports and the difficulty contemporary investigators had in tracking down first-hand witnesses suggests that many of these tales were of a type we today call urban legends. Nevertheless, a few of the attacks were certainly authentic, although whether these inspired the stories or were inspired *by* them is impossible to say. Whatever the underlying reality though, the grip of fear was undeniable.

For a time, just about any unsolved attack was automatically declared to be the work of this mysterious assailant. He – or it – was referred to by any of several names, including 'the Suburban Ghost' and 'the Leaping Terror'. But by February 1838, the newspapers were using the name we know today: Spring-Heeled Jack.

With his name now agreed upon, descriptions of Jack's appearance started to become more standardised. This was largely the result of two well-documented attacks, the first on 18-year-old Jane Alsop on 20 February 1838, and the second on Lucy Scales about a week later. (For a fuller account of Jack's exploits, interested readers are directed to the excellent study by Mike Dash – see the bibliography.)

'Hideous and frightful'

Jack was male, tall and thin, with a gaunt face and eyes that glowed like red balls of fire. There was some sort of large helmet on his head. He wore a voluminous black cloak, wrapped around a close-fitting garment of some shining material – possibly white oilskin. Blue and white fire crackled around his open mouth and he would vomit these flames directly into his victim's face. As for his hands, these were cold and hard, like claws. He was described in *The Times* of 22 February 1838 as 'hideous and frightful' to behold.

Other tales elaborated upon these details, sometimes giving Jack horns or cloven feet, peculiarly pointed ears or pale, corpse-like flesh. He was a terrifying figure indeed and was quickly adopted as a kind of national bogeyman. 'Be good,' children were warned, 'or Spring-Heeled Jack'll getcha.'

STRANGE MITCHAM

Spring-Heeled Jack comes to Mitcham

In her 1928 book, *Stand and Deliver*, Elizabeth Villiers records an incident (probably from 1838) in which horses bolted when a figure leapt across Streatham High Road, but it was to be another few decades before the seemingly immortal Spring-Heeled Jack made his first appearance in Mitcham itself.

In the late 1870s, Streatham Lane (now Road), leading north from Figges Marsh, was narrow and bordered with dense hedgerow. Tall elms arched overhead, their branches entwining into a canopy that hid the sun on even the brightest of summer days. After nightfall, the lonely lane was a genuinely creepy place, with only a handful of feeble oil lamps to relieve the pressing darkness, and silent save for the occasional hooting of owls and the sinister rustle of leaves.

(Above: looking north along Streatham Road today. Figges Marsh is on the left.)

The setting was perfect. Away from most shops and houses there was little chance of the villain being caught here and, for a while, any woman or child brave enough to venture down the lane at night risked a terrifying encounter with Jack. On several occasions, local doctors had to be called in to attend to Jack's victims but there do not seem to have been any injuries more serious than shock. Despite this, Mitcham's residents were seized by the same fear so many others had felt, and, before long, few dared leave their houses after nightfall.

Something had to be done and Sir Thomas Cato Worsfold records the efforts made by 'some of the stout lads of our village' to stage an ambush. In an essay that appears in Bidder's *Old Mitcham* Worsfold tells how these protectors of the peace disguised themselves in women's clothing and loitered around those areas that had seen most attacks, hoping to trick Jack into showing himself. They never did catch him, but it does seem that they successfully drove him away in the direction of Streatham Hill. Jack did not bother Mitcham again.

Who (or what) was Jack?

By the late 1880s, reports of Spring-Heeled Jack were becoming scarce (although even today they continue to trickle in from around the country). Possibly, his reputation was eclipsed by the more gruesome exploits of that other Jack, known as the Ripper.

So, who was Spring-Heeled Jack? There is no shortage of theories, many as bizarre as Jack himself.

To some, the original attacks were the work of a mad pieman who later committed suicide by jumping into the Thames before he was caught.

To others, he was a deformed (hence the red eyes) lunatic escaped from an asylum. Or perhaps an insane circus fire-eater / acrobat.

Author Peter Haining controversially claimed that the original perpetrator was a young Irish nobleman named Henry de la Poer Beresford, the Marquis of Waterford.

Even more colourful ideas range from a kangaroo (which had either been kept illegally as a pet and had got loose, or which had been dressed up by a mad animal trainer) to the idea put forward in 1961 that Jack was a UFO occupant.

Truthfully, nobody knows for sure. Many reported incidents were obviously no more than wild rumours, but there were some very real assaults as well. It also seems likely that there was more than one Jack at large. Several people were captured and brought to trial for impersonating him, yet the attacks went on. The length of time he was active supports the suggestion that his guise was assumed by more than one individual, but if there ever was an 'original' Spring-Heeled Jack, his identity remains shrouded in mystery. It is likely to remain that way forever.

Maiden Hill – A Lost Tumulus?

Did a large prehistoric monument once stand on Mitcham Common?

Some old maps of the common show a feature marked 'Maiden Hill', which seems to have been present up until at least the early 19th century. It stood near the junction of Beddington Lane and Croydon Road, ground now occupied by the golf course, but has since vanished. It may have been levelled when the golf course was constructed, or pulled apart to obtain gravel to build roads, but it is impossible to be certain as there are no historical records concerning its destruction.

Neither does history record what, if anything, the mound contained, although historians have commented that what appeared on the maps looked very much like a Bronze Age (c. 2100–700 BC) burial mound.

This interpretation is supported by the name 'Maiden', which Chambers Dictionary states is a 'common (though largely unexplained) name for a prehistoric earthwork'.

The Curse of Merton Priory

Hundreds of years ago Merton Priory stood there, a magnificent centre of worship straining up toward heaven. Today, the land is chiefly occupied by the Sainsbury's hypermarket (previously the 'Savacentre', built in 1988), but the priory still casts a shadow of sorts over the area.

Merton Priory belonged to the canons of St Augustine. Founded in AD 1114 by Gilbert the Norman, sheriff of Surrey, it was granted the manor of Merton by King Henry I in 1121, and for the next few hundred years the priory played an important role in English history. Between c.1130 and 1141, for example, Thomas Beckett (later Archbishop of Canterbury) was educated here. In 1217, peace terms between Henry III and Louis, Dauphin of France were confirmed here. When Parliament met here in 1236, two decades after the signing of *Magna Carta*, the resulting *Statute of Merton* became the first written declaration on points of law, seeing the birth of modern parliamentary democracy. And in 1437 King Henry VI was crowned here.

But in 1534 King Henry VIII assumed leadership of the Church in England and dissolved the country's monasteries, taking their wealth for himself. Merton Priory was surrendered in 1538, and its destruction began almost at once, the rubble being taken away to be used in the construction of other buildings, such as Nonsuch Palace near Cheam. Some of the remains may also have been used later in the construction of a much nearer building (see the chapter on 'Everett's Place').

Today, little can be seen here of the once-magnificent Priory although its remains were briefly exposed during excavations undertaken when the hypermarket was being built. The only remains visible on the site today are the foundations of the Chapter House (preserved inside a specially constructed room beneath Merantun Way – shown below – and occasionally made accessible to the public) and some stretches of the precinct walls.

Following the dissolution of the monasteries, a popular belief spread that taking ownership of old church land – land that rightfully belonged to God – brought dire consequences. This gave rise to a number of stories of cursed land, and it is not surprising that the important site of Merton Priory should feature in one such tradition. In *The Natural History and Antiquities of the County of Surrey*, Volume 1, (1718–19), John Aubrey wrote that, since the 'sacrilegious Dissolution' this site 'has been generally observ'd fatal to its Possessors.'

The antiquary Sir Henry Spelman had recorded this superstition in his *History and Fate of Sacrilege* (first published in 1698) and his book was updated in the 1840s by two anonymous Church of England priests, and again in 1888 by Samuel Eales.

Eales and the priests gave detailed histories of old church sites, listing the frequent changes in ownership. They argued that most people who took possession of these sites fell into hardship, rarely holding onto the land long enough to pass it to their sons, and that this fact constituted proof that the land was cursed.

Eales's book records that the site of Merton Priory was granted to Gregory Lovel, Nicholas Zouch and Thomas Ware in 1586. They sold it in 1601 to Charles, earl of Nottingham, who conveyed it in 1604 to John Spilman, who in turn conveyed it in 1606 to Sir Thomas Cornwallis. The entry continues in this manner for some considerable time, coming eventually to Sir William Phippard who died in 1723, leaving it to his sons. Unfortunately, Phippard's sons all died childless and so the estate passed by marriage to R.F. Mansfield in about 1780. This is the last transaction the author records.

His entry concludes: 'In two hundred years we have twenty-one possessors and eighteen families; the estate only twice descending from father to son.'

He then gives similar details for the Priory's estates at Dunsfold, Kingswood, Ewell and Shelwood, making the same argument.

More recently, Evelyn M. Jowett referred to this curse in *An Illustrated History of Merton and Morden* (1951), stating: 'This superstition to which the all too frequent changes in ownership of local estates might well have given rise among the villagers, was of course due to the curious failure of male heirs among nearly all the local gentry of Merton for centuries past.'

(Above: part of the medieval precinct wall still visible in Station Road, Merton.)

In 1999, the story was updated when it appeared on the front page of the local *Independent* newspaper. Now, the curse was being blamed for problems with what was then the car park / waste ground at Merton Abbey Mills, where 'huge potholes' and 'gaping ruts' were causing damage to cars.

If there is a curse then some might suggest that its greatest victim is the site itself, which despite its historic significance rarely receives the attention it deserves.

The 'Triple L'

Shortly after he founded the Travel and Earth Mysteries Society (TEMS) in 1992, Lionel Beer noticed how a number of ancient sites to the south-west of London appeared to fall in a line running almost west to east. Colleagues practised in the art of dowsing (searching for hidden objects or energy, often with the aid of pendulums, forked twigs or dowsing rods) later confirmed that he had discovered a ley line and the alignment was named the 'Triple L', standing for 'Lionel's Ley Line'.

STRANGE MITCHAM

First identified by Arthur Watkins in The Old Straight Track (1925), ley lines (or simply leys) are said to be straight lines that connect ancient, often sacred, sites. Watkins's ideas were later enlarged upon by the New Age movement, which linked these leys with the concept of lines of energy running through the Earth.

At the western end of the 'Triple L' is an old church in Littleton, Shepperton, built on a site that has seen a church standing for over a thousand years. From there the line heads east, passing through the Diana Fountain in Bushy Park (designed by Sir Christopher Wren and dedicated to the Roman goddess Diana) and entering Kingston-upon-Thames at the Bishop Out of Residence public house beside the river, built on the site of the old Bishop's Palace. The ley then passes through the site of the Saxon chapel of St Mary, which once abutted All Saints Parish Church beside Kingston's market place and which may have been the original home of the town's Coronation Stone.

A short distance to the east, Kingston's Lovekyn chantry chapel, built in 1309, also stands on the line and continuing still further east the line passes through the church of St Peter in Norbiton and a church at Cottenham Park before narrowly missing the church of St John the Divine in High Path, Merton. (It passes just to the south of this church, across the junction of Merantun Way and Morden Road.) It then crosses the River Wandle and passes through the grounds of Merton Priory before continuing on towards Crystal Palace Park.

One Legend Too Many

In the original edition of *Strange Mitcham* I mentioned that the body of King Henry I had lain in state at Merton Priory following his death in 1135. However, according to Lionel Green in his excellent 2005 book, *A Priory Revealed using material relating to Merton Priory*, this is not true, despite the claim being given as fact in numerous publications.

It would appear that, in writing about local legends, I inadvertently included one legend more than I had intended!

Everett's Place

As mentioned in the preceding chapter ('The Curse of Merton Priory'), much of the rubble from that great building was recycled and used in the construction of other places, such as Nonsuch Palace. It is likely that some also found its way into the building materials of a rather unusual structure located a short distance to the south of the Priory.

Standing at the top of Phipps Bridge Road is what at first glance appears to be a ruined castle. Here, a single round tower, its upper section overgrown and seemingly crumbled with age, stands watch over the parked cars. Blank arrow slits stare blindly from the wall, while a dark arched window lies in shadow beneath foliage-clad battlements. The tower feels ancient and strangely out of place in its surroundings.

But a closer look reveals missed details. That tower looks sturdier than it should, as if it were deliberately designed to look time-ravaged. The arch and arrow-slits conceal comfortable glass windows. The whole structure begins to seem more like a folly – one of those once-fashionable fake ruins that embellished many a gentleman's garden in the late 18th and early 19th centuries. Yet even follies were nothing but empty shells whereas this tower was obviously built to be lived in.

It stands at the northern end of a row of five cottages called 'Everett's Place'. The first four of these cottages were built in 1824 by Henry Everett. The fifth was added at a later date, possibly later in the 1820s or in the 1830s. Whatever the exact year was, records show that all five cottages were standing by July 1870. There was no tower yet though.

That was erected a few years later. Local tradition has it that, by the 1870s, the fifth cottage was already in danger of collapse due to settlement. Understandably, the cottage's owners were anxious to prevent this and in about 1875 they came up with the novel idea of buttressing the ailing building with the folly we see today.

At the same time, the owners seem to have decided that the folly should contain a compact cottage suitable for an extra tenant. Perhaps they reasoned that the additional income would help recoup the money spent on the building work.

Given its unusual (but highly attractive) appearance it is not surprising that a number of stories have circulated over the years concerning the source of the materials used in this stone, flint and brick tower. One such story is that the rubble came from the site of Merton Priory, which stood less than half a mile [0.8 kilometres] away. For a long time after its destruction, local builders used the Priory's remains as a handy quarry, and historians concede that this theory is quite likely to be correct.

(It has also been suggested that the tower was designed to resemble the Priory's old gatehouse but there is no evidence to support this.)

If the Priory's remains really were used here, it may not be a very good place to live if you are superstitious. During the 19th century it was popularly believed that it was unlucky to reuse building materials from monasteries and churches. (There was a similar belief regarding the land on which the monasteries originally stood – see the chapter on 'The Curse of Merton Priory'.) Fortunately though, there do not appear to have been any tales of misfortune caused by the tower.

Other claims regarding the building materials dispute the Priory theory. One alternative story is that the workers included masonry rubble from old gravel pits, and that these were the same pits that had been used to dump debris from the medieval London Bridge. Therefore, this story goes, the tower is all that now survives of that famous old bridge.

Another belief is that the materials came from the Tower of London and that the building was designed the way it was in imitation of one of the Tower's guardrooms. And yet another belief is that the stone came from the nearby estate of Lord Nelson.

However, historians consider these last three theories unlikely to be true.

In 2006, a relative of someone who used to live in the tower told me that her family had believed the building to be haunted. I recorded this in *Mysterious Mitcham*.

UFOs over Mitcham

Mitcham has never been called a UFO 'hotspot', so I was mildly surprised at the number of reports I found while researching *Strange Mitcham*. First though, a word of caution.

When considering UFOs it is important to remember that the 'U' stands for 'Unidentified'. The term is not and should not be synonymous with 'flying saucer' or 'alien spacecraft' (although it is not entirely impossible that some UFOs are precisely that). In any case, 'UFO' is the label given to such a diverse group of phenomena that no single explanation can underlie all sightings.

What follows then is simply a collection of reports of strange things seen in the skies over Mitcham. They are, by definition, unidentified flying objects.

The 1980s

In 1983 the *Mitcham News* carried a report about a 'potato-shaped' object seen gliding across the skyline on the evening of Monday 15 August. It had appeared at about 8.30 p.m. as the skies were darkening, and a police spokesman later stated that the station had received several telephone calls from alarmed members of the public. Confusingly, this spokesman claimed the UFO was probably the result of shooting stars, which seems unlikely given that shooting stars invariably zip across the sky, appear as bright points of light and do not tend to resemble vegetables.

Two months later, the same newspaper printed a letter from Mrs V Lyons, who had seen a pair of unusual lights on Friday 14 October, at some time between 7.50 and 8.05 p.m.

She had been walking across Cranmer Green towards the Canons when she spotted the lights 'swaying from left to right coming towards me from the direction of London.'

It was not until she read a tabloid article a few days afterwards that she interpreted what she had seen as a UFO, but when she did she felt 'excited that [she] could have seen one over Mitcham!'

The 1997 wave of sightings

Throughout September and October 1997, there was a wave of UFO reports from all across the London Borough of Merton.

The first witness was a lady living near Morden Hall Park, an insomniac who regularly stays awake until the early hours of the morning.

At 4.40 a.m. on 6 September, she saw a large and very bright white light apparently hovering and dancing over a tree in the park, near Morden Lodge. Being used to staring out of the window while unable to sleep, the lady was familiar with the night sky and knew that this light was well away from the usual aeroplane flight-paths. Puzzled, she watched it perform for some time until it finally 'went backwards at a terrific speed and got smaller and smaller'.

The following morning the light was back. This time, the lady woke her husband (who was not best pleased at being dragged out of bed so early) and they both watched the light dance around for a while before it shot off sideways, followed by a second light. Neither witness could explain what they had seen and so the lady got in touch with Ann Hopkins, a member of the Travel and Earth Mysteries Society (TEMS).

After learning of these sightings, Ann wrote a letter to her local newspaper appealing for further information. She was quickly contacted by a reporter who told her he had received another UFO report from the same week. The reporter decided to write an article on the sightings and this appeared on 9 October, under the heading 'UFO sightings excite experts'.

The article gave Ann Hopkins's telephone number and, over the next few days, she received some 20 further reports. The continuing interest led to a second article – 'Number of UFO sightings rises' – being published on 23 October.

Had the media hype simply stirred up people's imaginations – this was, after all, at the height of *The X-Files* television show's popularity – or was there something more bizarre going on?

At about 8 p.m. on 1 October, a lady was walking across Mitcham Common with her son and daughter when they saw a bright light in the sky above them. They described the light as orange and said that it seemed to have a cross in the centre of it.

On 8 October, at about 5.15 in the evening, a worker at St George's Hospital in Tooting watched a silvery oval-shaped object fly through the sky. Later that same evening, a woman in Belvedere Square in Wimbledon saw a round crimson light hover above some trees before flying away.

One of the new reports was particularly interesting because of the date. At about 4 a.m. on the morning of 7 September, a man and his wife had seen a bright white light hovering over King's College School (by the Ridgway in Wimbledon). The light was so bright, they said, that it lit up the surrounding area.

This was the same morning that the original witness – the insomniac lady – had watched a bright white light in Morden Hall Park for the second time. Morden Hall Park is only about one mile [one-and-a-half kilometres] south-east of King's College School and it is tempting to believe that these are independent sightings of the same object.

By November 1997, there had been 27 reports of UFOs from Morden, Wimbledon, Tooting and Mitcham. People had seen unidentified red lights, green lights and white lights. Some lights had held together, others had had 'bits' break off them and fall to earth. A few people came forward to report actual structured craft. One man had apparently seen a craft 'the size of a house' hovering over a Wimbledon recreation ground. Another woman told how she and her husband had seen a solid, low-domed craft hover over the flats opposite their Wimbledon home some five years earlier.

1999–2002

As is the nature of these waves, things died down and nothing else seems to have been reported from around here until *UFO Magazine* printed a letter in their March / April 2000 issue. This was from Wimbledon resident John Beadle, aged 61, reporting seeing a strange triangular-shaped craft at 1.20 a.m. on 17 November 1999.

The craft was a light, smoky grey colour, about 10 feet (three metres) long. It had rounded corners, a red light in the centre of the underbelly, and white lights along the edges. At the rear there was a very bright white light. The object passed right over Mr Beadle's head in complete silence, the incident lasting between two and three minutes – plenty of time for him to get a good look at it.

A few months later, another UFO sighting was reported, this time in *The Wimbledon, Morden and Mitcham Independent* newspaper. This took place on Sunday 20 February 2000, near the site of Merton Priory, only about three-quarters of a mile [one kilometre] from Mr Beadle's sighting. At around noon Ronald John, a 39-year-old electronics development engineer, was driving east along Merantun Way with his wife's friend and three children. As they neared the Savacentre (now Sainsbury's) hypermarket they all saw a bright flashing light high in the sky ahead of them.

They were so intrigued that they parked the car in a nearby road and just stared up at this light. It was egg-shaped, larger than any star would have been (even if a star would have been visible at noon) and was coloured bright silver at the top with a deep red colour at the base. Anxious to confirm what they could see, Mr John even stopped a passer-by to ask if he could see it too. He could.

After hanging motionless in the air for some 10 minutes, the light abruptly shot upward at 'amazing speed', shrinking in apparent size until it resembled a small star. It was finally obscured from view when a cloud passed in front of it. It has been suggested that the physical description of this UFO matches that of a metallic-foil helium-filled party balloon, but the witnesses were certain that its movements ruled this explanation out.

STRANGE MITCHAM

2004

In September 2004 Della Edwards and her boyfriend Paul Ferman saw what Della called a 'massive ball of light' in the sky over Mitcham Common. It was white, 'brighter than the moon' and appeared to be at about rooftop level.

'It didn't have a solid shape,' Della told me in 2007. 'It was round but with no solid lines. I think the best way to explain it is like a flashing moon up close, but as if someone had smudged or brushed the [circular] lines outwards to light up the sky.'

She described the flashing as fast, resembling a strobe light and Paul remembered that there was 'a slight lightning effect to it (yellowy / green)'.

For a fuller account of this incident, see my *Mysterious Mitcham*.

An Identified Flying Object

The vast majority of UFO sightings can eventually be explained, given enough information and investigation. The classic flying saucer seen over Mitcham in 1994 is a good example of this.

In September of that year, workers travelling home from shops, factories and offices stopped and stared at the sky in amazement. What was crossing silently over their heads appeared to have come straight from a science-fiction film.

Witness Philip Shaw gave a description of the UFO to the local *Guardian* newspaper: 'It was saucer-shaped, bigger than a plane and very bright.'

Another witness – a lady who wished to remain anonymous – had been visiting friends and was driving home with her husband and 27-year-old daughter when all three of them saw the mysterious object.

'We saw this light looming ahead of us as bright as the moon,' she told a journalist. 'My husband said jokingly it was a flying saucer. We all had a good laugh but as we got closer we couldn't believe our eyes.'

Scores of other witnesses described the same sight – a large, glowing, orange saucer-shaped object that slid slowly through the air. Not surprisingly, many came to the conclusion that they had seen a craft from another planet.

Sceptical *Guardian* staff were less sure however, and their investigation soon revealed the likely culprit. It seems that the flying saucer had actually been a luminous Virgin airship flying south from Wembley Stadium as it returned to its base.

So that explains one of the objects seen over Mitcham. As for the others, that 'U' in UFO continues to apply....

Afterword

When I was originally researching *Strange Mitcham* I unearthed far more material than could be included. Back in 2002 the economics of printing meant that the length of the finished booklet had to be limited in order to keep the price down to a reasonable level.

I therefore had to cut out a number of stories that I had wanted to tell, stories such as the legendary origins of Mitcham's famous annual fair, the ghostly sightings to the south of Mitcham Common and the magical tree that could cure whooping cough. I kept these stories on file however, and as people started to read *Strange Mitcham* and contact me with tales of their own I quickly amassed enough material to put together a sequel to *Strange Mitcham*, which I called *Mysterious Mitcham*.

For more details about *Mysterious Mitcham*, as well as my other writings, please visit my website at www.james-clark.co.uk.

I hope you have enjoyed reading these tales as much as I enjoyed finding out about them, and that the next time you find yourself walking through this old town it feels just that little bit stranger than it did before.

Best wishes,

James Clark (January 2011)

Appendix: The Southend Murderer

(See the chapter on 'The Haunting of Rose Cottage'.)

James Canham Read was handsome, charming and a ladies' man. In 1892 he was involved with three women. As well as his wife in Stepney (with whom he had eight children), he was having one affair with Miss Florence Dennis and another with Miss Beatrice Kempton. Unfortunately, Beatrice fell pregnant in October 1893. Unable to marry her, Read somehow persuaded her to live with him as 'Mr and Mrs Edgar Benson'. Their baby was born in January 1894, and early that year they rented a bed-sitting room in Rose Cottage in Mitcham.

But Read's triple life was crippling him. He was spending a fortune travelling, entertaining Florrie, maintaining one real wife and one pretend wife, and feeding and clothing a total of nine children. Then, to make matters worse, he learned that Florrie was pregnant too! Florrie's shocked mother sent her away to live with her sister, Mrs Louisa Ayriss, at Southend. (Presumably, her mother did not know that Read had also already had an affair with Louisa several years before!) Once there, Florrie sent Read a telegram, asking what 'arrangements' he would be making for her. More money worries....

Something must have finally snapped for it seems that Read killed Florrie on the night of 24 June. Her body was found in a watery ditch at Prittlewell, about two miles [three kilometres] from Southend. She had been shot once in the head, from so close that the wound was blackened with gunpowder.

On his return to London, Read stole £159.12s.6d. from his employers and abandoned his real identity, intending to live out the rest of his life as Edgar Benson with his 'darling Beatty' in Mitcham. However, he was eventually tracked down and arrested at Rose Cottage by Detective Inspector Baker of Scotland Yard.

The trial of 'The Southend Murderer' was a sensation, but in the end the jury took just half an hour to find him guilty. James Canham Read was hanged at Springfield Prison in Chelmsford on 4 December 1894.

Further Reading

By the same author – see www.james-clark.co.uk for details:

Mysterious Mitcham

The sequel to *Strange Mitcham*: more ghosts, legends and mysteries of Mitcham in Surrey / south London

Haunted Wandsworth

Ghosts and legends of the London Borough of Wandsworth (covers Balham, Battersea, Putney, Tooting and Wandsworth)

Haunted London

Ghosts and legends of Central London

Readers may also be interested in the following titles:

Mysterious Wimbledon and *More Mysterious Wimbledon*

By Ruth Murphy and Clive Whichelow, Enigma Publishing

Strange Kingston and *Mysterious Kingston*

By Barbara and Tracy Russell, Twilight Books

Strange Croydon

By Valerie Hope, online at www.rwhit.dsl.pipex.com

Selected Bibliography

Books, magazines, etc.

Arnold, F. (1886) *The History of Streatham*, Elliot Stock, London.

Aubrey, J. (1718-19) *The Natural History and Antiquities of the County of Surrey*, Volume 1, 1975 edition, Kohler and Coombes, Dorking.

Beer, L. (2009) 'The Lovekyn Chapel and the Triple L', *eTEMSNews* 14, Summer 2009, Travel and Earth Mysteries Society.

Begg, P. (1981) 'The terror of London', *The Unexplained* No. 39, Orbis Publishing Ltd, London. pp.770–773.

Bidder, Lt.-Col. H. F. (DSO), (1926) *Old Mitcham: A series of papers recording village life and history, Part II*, H. G. Mather, Mitcham.

Brown, J. W. (1996) *Notes on Mitcham from The Gentleman's Magazine*, Local History Reprints, Streatham. (Letter from 'E.I.C.' reprinted from *The Gentleman's Magazine*, 1821, Part II, pp.17–20.)

Bruce, P. and Mason, S. (1993) *Merton Priory*, jointly published by the Museum of London Archaeology Service and the London Borough of Merton.

Chamberlain, W. H. (1925) *Reminiscences of Old Merton*, Mitchell Hughes and Clarke, London.

Clark, J. (2002) *Strange Mitcham*, 1st edition, Shadowtime Publishing, Mitcham.

Clark, J. (2006) *Haunted Wandsworth*, The History Press (was Tempus Publishing), Stroud, Gloucestershire.

Dash, M. (1996) 'Spring-heeled Jack – to Victorian bugaboo from suburban ghost', *Fortean Studies* Volume 3, John Brown Publishing, London.

Denbigh, K. (1975) *History and Heroes of Old Merton*, Charles Skilton Ltd, London.

Francis, T. *Old Mitcham*, lecture notes, held at Merton Local Studies Centre.

Francis, T. (1993) *Old Mitcham*, edited by E. Montague, Phillimore and Co. Ltd, Sussex.

Green, L. (2005) *A Priory Revealed using material relating to Merton Priory*, Merton Historical Society in association with Merton Priory Trust.

Haining, P. (1977) *The Legend and Bizarre Crimes of Spring Heeled Jack*, Frederick Muller Ltd, London.

Hopkins, A. (1997) 'UFOs over Merton', *TEMS News* 17, Travel and Earth Mysteries Society.

Jowett, E .M. (1951) *An Illustrated History of Merton and Morden*, Festival of Britain Local Committee.

Lysons, Rev D. (AM, FAS) (1792) *The Environs of London: Being an Historical Account of the Towns, Villages and Hamlets, Within Twelve Miles of that Capital: Interspersed with Biographical Anecdotes, Volume the First, County of Surrey*, reprinted as *Lysons's History of Mitcham*, compiled by Brown, J.W. (1991), Local History Reprints, Streatham.

Meller, H. (1994) *London Cemeteries: An Illustrated Guide and Gazetteer*, 3rd edition, Scolar Press, Aldershot.

Montague, E. (1970) *The History of Mitcham Common*, The Mitcham Common Preservation Society.

Montague, E. (1976) *The 'Canons' Mitcham*, Merton Historical Society.

Montague, E. (1988/89) *Three Kings*.

Montague, E. (1991) *Mitcham, A Pictorial History*, Sussex, Phillimore and Co. Ltd, Sussex.

Montague, E. (1992) *A Guide to the Parish Church of St. Peter and St. Paul, Mitcham, Surrey*.

Montague, E. (1992), *The Archaeology of Mitcham*, Merton Historical Society.

Montague, E. (1995) *Phipp's Bridge*.

Montague, E. (1995) *Ravensbury*.

Murphy, R. and Whichelow, C. (1995) *More Mysterious Wimbledon*, Enigma Publishing, Wimbledon.

Spelman, Sir H. (1698) *The History and Fate of Sacrilege*, (Eales, S.L. edition, 1888, John Hodges).

Villiers, E. (1928) *Stand and Deliver: The Romantic Adventures of Certain Gentlemen of the High Toby, Their Times, Their Associates, Friends and Victims*, Stanley Paul and Co. Ltd, London.

Walford, E. (1884) *Greater London: A Narrative of its History, its People, and its Places*, Volumes I and II, Cassell and Co. Ltd, London, Paris and New York.

Watkins, A. (1925) *The Old Straight Track*, Methuen.

Worsfold, Sir T. C., Bart. 'Memories of our Village', in Bidder, Lt.-Col. H. F. (DSO), (1926) *Old Mitcham: A series of papers recording village life and history, Part II*, H. G. Mather, Mitcham.

Websites

'British Archaeology Magazine', #44, May 1999, 'Tolerating pagans for the sake of trade', by P Blinkhorn, at www.britarch.ac.uk/ba/ba44/ba44feat.html (accessed January 2011).

'Mysterious Mitcham' by James Clark, at www.shadowtimepublishing.co.uk (accessed January 2011).

'Obiwan's UFO-Free Paranormal Page', at http://ufofreeparanormal.com/node/23 (accessed January 2011).

'O'Neill's Ghostories Casements Library', at www.ghostories.com/casement.htm (accessed January 2011).

Newspaper articles and letters

'Close encounters perplex residents', *Mitcham and Morden Guardian*, 15 September 1994.

'Curse of the stones', *Wimbledon, Morden and Mitcham Independent*, 20 May 1999.

'Did I see a UFO?', letter from Mrs V Lyons, *Mitcham News*, 21 October 1983.

'Ghost Stories of Old Mitcham – Spring-Heeled Jack and Lady Jane: The Well at Rose Cottage', *Mitcham News and Mercury*, 28 December 1951.

'Mitcham Notes', by 'The Commoner', *Mitcham and Tooting Advertiser*, 9 September 1943.

'Mystery of flying object is solved', *Mitcham and Morden Guardian*, 22 September 1994.

'Potato shaped UFO!', *Mitcham News*, 19 August 1983.

'Rose Cottage Was Not Always So Quiet', by P. Wilson, *The News*, 4 September 1959.

'Secret passage was an escape route', M. Exell, *The News*, 20 February 1959.

'The Experiencers!' *UFO Magazine*, March / April 2000.

'The Southend Murder: Arrest of Read', *The Daily Chronicle*, 9 July 1894.

'The truth is out there…somewhere', *Wimbledon, Morden and Mitcham Independent*, 24 February 2000.

'Tribal burial is true story', letter from F Cain, Member of the Romany Guild, *Mitcham News*, 12 February 1982.

Index

STRANGE MITCHAM

Lightning Source UK Ltd.
Milton Keynes UK
UKHW012143230919

·350303UK00002B/752/P